Sapphics and Uncertainties

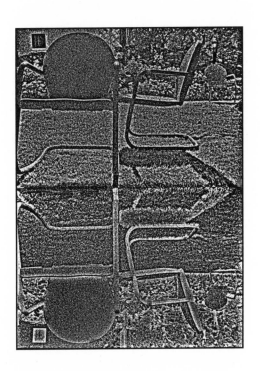

Sapphics and Uncertainties

POEMS
1970–1986

TIMOTHY STEELE

THE UNIVERSITY OF ARKANSAS PRESS
FAYETTEVILLE 1995

99   98   97   96   95   5   4   3   2   1

Designed by Gail Carter

⊗ The paper used in this publication meets the
minimum requirements of the American
National Standard for Permanence of Paper for
Printed Library Materials Z39.48-1984.

Library of Congress Cataloging-in-Publication Data
Steele, Timothy.
     Sapphics   and   uncertainties : poems   1970–1986   /
Timothy Steele.
        p.   cm.
     ISBN 1-55728-376-1 (alk. paper). —
     ISBN 1-55728-375-3 (pbk. : alk. paper)
     I. Title.
PS3569.T33845S3   1995
811'.54—dc20   95-6846
                                            CIP

Grateful acknowledgment is made to the following journals, in
which some of these poems first appeared: *Canto, Chicago Review,
Chowder Review, Classical Outlook, Counter/Measures, The Epigram-
matist, Gramercy Review, Greensboro Review, Nebo, Occident, Paris
Review, PN Review* (England), *Sequoia, Southern Humanities Review,
Southern Poetry Review, Southern Review, Threepenny Review,* and
TriQuarterly. "Three Notes Toward Definitions," "Angel,"
"Chanson Philosophique," "The Chorus," and "On the Eve of a
Birthday" were initially published in *Poetry,* copyright 1977, 1982,
and 1983 by the Modern Poetry Association.
     Other poems appeared in the following limited editions: *The
Prudent Heart* (Symposium Press), *Nine Poems* (Robert L. Barth),
On Harmony (Abattoir Editions), and *Short Subjects* (Robert L. Barth).

CONTENTS

Uncertainties
and Rest

1979

PREFACE

This volume returns to print my first two collections of poems. The second appears as it did originally, but for a couple of minor adjustments of wording and punctuation. From the earlier book, however, I have dropped seven poems, have made three substitutions in the sequence of epigrams, and have in several other places altered lines or passages that seemed, on my re-reading of them, to be weak or unnecessarily obscure.

Making these changes, and contemplating others that I eventually decided against, I felt as most poets must when they re-issue early work. While not wanting to be disloyal to the poems, I wished to spare the reader those which had not worn well. And though I was concerned about violating the original process of composition, it seemed reasonable to correct glitches which were merely incidental to a poem's meaning or structure. Ultimately, I tried to steer a course between overindulgence and excessive severity—between the inclination to let be and the impulse to tinker and retrench—in hopes that the resulting compromise would faithfully serve the claims of both the past and the present.

I should like to thank for their kind support Beverly Jarrett, who edited *Uncertainties and Rest* when it was published by Louisiana State University Press, and Anne Freedgood, who edited *Sapphics against Anger and Other Poems* for Random House. And I should especially like to thank Miller Williams for his interest in this current volume.

Sapphics against Anger
and Other Poems

1986

For Vikram Seth

We enter life and thus inherit
The kingdom of the human voice.
The Word is Word because we share it.
Wonder encourages our choice
To sort out life's conflicting data,
To come to terms with its traumata,
To shape ourselves to nothing less
Than reasoned self-forgetfulness.
For years we've traded rhyme and measure,
And if our poems are books today,
It is in hopes that others may
Take from them solace, sense, or pleasure,
Though years pass with their wonted speed
And though the times we shared recede.

FROM A ROOFTOP

At dawn, down in the streets, from pavement grills,
Steam rises like the spent breath of the night.
At open windows, curtains stir on sills;
There's caging drawn across a market's face;
An empty crane, at its construction site,
Suspends a cable into chasmed space.

The roof shows other rooftops, their plateaus
Marked with antennas from which lines are tied
And strung with water beads or hung with clothes.
And here and there a pigeon comes to peck
At opaque puddles, its stiff walk supplied
By herky-jerky motions of its neck.

Downtown, tall buildings surmount a thinning haze.
The newest, the world center of a bank,
Has sides swept upward from a block-broad base,
Obsidian glass, fifty stories tall;
Against it hangs a window-washer's plank,
An aerie on a frozen waterfall.

Nearer and eastward, past still-sleeping blocks,
Crews on the waterfront are changing shifts.
Trucks load at warehouses at the foot of docks;
A tug out in the bay, gathering speed,
With a short hollow blast of puffed smoke, lifts
Gulls to a cawing and air-borne stampede.

It is as if dawn pliantly compels
The city to relax to sounds and shapes,
To its diagonals and parallels:
Long streets with traffic signals blinking red,
Small squares of parks, alleys with fire escapes,
Rooftops above which cloudless day is spread.

And it's as if the roofs' breeze-freshened shelves,
Their level surfaces of graveled tar
Where glassy fragments glitter, are themselves
A measure of the intermediate worth
Of all the stories to the morning star
And all the stories to the morning earth.

THE SHEETS

From breezeway or through front porch screen
You'd see the sheets, wide blocks of white
Defined against a backdrop of
A field whose grasses were a green
    Intensity of light.

How fresh they looked there on the line,
Their laundered sweetness through the hours
Gathering richly in the air
While cumulus clouds gathered in
    Topheavily piled towers.

We children tightroped the low walls
Along the garden; bush and bough
And the washed sheets moved in the wind;
And thinking of this now recalls
    Vasari's tale of how

Young Leonardo, charmed of sight,
Would buy in the loud marketplace
Caged birds and set them free—thus yielding
Back to the air which gave him light
    Lost beauty and lost grace.

So with the sheets: for as they drew
Clear warming sunlight from the sky,
They gave to light their rich, clean scent.
And when, the long day nearly through,
    My cousin Anne and I

Would take the sheets down from the line,
We'd fold in baskets their crisp heat,
Absorbing, as they had, the fine
Steady exchange of earth and sky,
    Material and sweet.

SNAPSHOTS FOR POSTERITY

Already the infant
Has turned towards
Those grandly situated
Between memory
And anticipation—
Past and future—upon
The moving edge of time.

O little sausage legs,
Unsteadily
Padding the floor,
You pause,
And your fingers clutch
And release the air
In unblinking wonderment.

May you one day chant,
"Vanity, vanity,"
As a charm against
The chartering of hopes,
The illusory ports
Of wares and commerce.
Then, lucky child,

Even shutting the album
Upon the past will be
An act of devotion,
A paternoster
Accommodating
The fluid present,
Apt in all circumstance.

OLD LETTERS

Old letters are reproaches, mute petitions
    Unlosable in some desk drawer
Or attic box. Bunched in brown folders, or
In packets tied with ribbon, they speak of
    Now-jettisoned ambitions
And insecurities which passed for love,
And document not times when we were stronger,
But rather climates favorable to
Illusions not illusions any longer.

Thus they appear to warn us to adjust
    Our self-important postures; and
One may, of a warm summer evening, stand
Reading them in a room where gold light falls,
    In shafts aswim with dust,
Across a floor to flowery-papered walls;
And as one reads, one may, between the lines,
Construct the features of a former self
Too given to the self and its designs.

Likewise, to return the letters finally
    Back to wherever they belong
Is to admit how much of life's gone wrong
Because of vanity and discontent,
    And is as well to envy
Those who refuse to hunger for event
And who accept the wisely unbegun,
Just wishing decently to get through life
And trying not to injure anyone.

SMALL LIVES

Having explored the oddly solar weather
Inside a lampshade, the dazed fly will tire,
Drop to the desk, and rub front legs together
As though to warm itself before a fire.

Capsizing with a shovelful of peat,
A pill bug wobbles on its back with fear:
It works its numerous and frantic feet,
Then curls its segments up into a sphere.

The topsoil or the manuscript can wait:
I plant my spade or break off in mid-phrase.
If asked why such small lives so fascinate,
Why I observe them, I can't really tell.
But a responsive impulse moves my gaze,
An impulse I can see in them as well.

MOCKINGBIRD

Erratically, tirelessly, in song,
He does his imitations all day long.
Appropriating every voice he hears,
Astonishingly shifting vocal gears,
He chirrups, trills, and whistles crazily,
Perched at the twiggy apex of his tree.

When argued with by smaller, lesser birds,
He raucously refutes them with their words;
When not receiving notice, as he should,
From earthbound members of the neighborhood
He drops down on to chimney or garage,
Continuing his hectoring barrage.

One might object to his inflated noise,
The pertinacious manner he employs,
Except the sequences which he invents
Are born of urgent pathos, in this sense:
For all his virtuosity of tone,
The singer has no note which is his own.

JANET

Wading away from shore,
We skirt a cloud of midges.
A small-scale desert floor,
The bottom is a smoothed
Expanse of wavy ridges,
Occasionally cross-grooved

Where a clam's left its path.
We scoop from the calm lake
A brisk adaptive bath,
My legs like milky stalks
In water, and a wake
Spreading where Janet walks.

We're twelve, and evening leaves
Me edgy and nonplussed:
Her tight red swimsuit sheathes
Slim hips, small breasts, and serves
To shape a figure just
Developing its curves.

The lake's inched up our suits.
Drawing a breath of air,
She sinks, frog kicks, and shoots
Sleekly across the sand,
Beneath the surface where
Her hair was briefly fanned.

LIFE PORTRAIT

thinking of Dora Spenlow and David Copperfield

Her pensive figure charms, as does the lisp
And coaxing baby talk she sometimes plies.
Yet his devotion wanes. What beckons him?
    The customary will-o'-the-wisp—
A dreamed-up soul mate, beautiful and wise?
No matter: what it comes to, in the end,
Is that when in mock-plaintive moments she
Says, "Don't forget, bad boy, your little friend,"
He fails to catch the import of the plea.

She dies; in time he marries his ideal,
And forges to success. Yet the detail
Of his fulfillment never quite convinces.
    And it's her presence he will feel
Hiking up switchbacks of a mountain trail.
The daffodil, bowed at the canyon's rim,
Will drop a bead of water like a note
From its toy trumpet blossom, his eyes will swim,
And he'll feel a thick hot tightness in his throat.

He's one, now, with the greedy overreachers.
She sat, hands on his shoulder, chin on them,
Then ran a thoughtful finger down his profile,
    As if to remind him of his features.
Height shows the small lake as a sparkling gem,
And shows as threads the streams that spill and bend
And join and part along the valley's floor.
He once forgot, bad boy, his little friend,
Although he won't forget her any more.

SAPPHICS AGAINST ANGER

Angered, may I be near a glass of water;
May my first impulse be to think of Silence,
Its deities (who are they? do, in fact, they
        Exist? etc.).

May I recall what Aristotle says of
The subject: to give vent to rage is not to
Release it but to be increasingly prone
        To its incursions.

May I imagine being in the *Inferno,*
Hearing it asked: "Virgilio mio, who's
That sulking with Achilles there?" and hearing
        Virgil say: "Dante,

That fellow, at the slightest provocation,
Slammed phone receivers down, and waved his arms like
A madman. What Attila did to Europe,
        What Genghis Khan did

To Asia, that poor dope did to his marriage."
May I, that is, put learning to good purpose,
Mindful that melancholy is a sin, though
        Stylish at present.

Better than rage is the post-dinner quiet,
The sink's warm turbulence, the streaming platters,
The suds rehearsing down the drain in spirals
        In the last rinsing.

For what is, after all, the good life save that
Conducted thoughtfully, and what is passion
If not the holiest of powers, sustaining
        Only if mastered.

1816

Forest-swelled winds, all night, surge round
The cabin; hugely, trees go wild
Above deep-troughed, snowdrifted ground.
Inside, in front of the fireplace,
Firelight on his stubbled face
And long-sleeved undershirt, the man
Watches his wife, whose woolen form
Bends to the cradle of a child
Wailing against each blast of storm.

Nor can the child be comforted.
He cannot guess the storm will end
Or that in time he will be led
To the mad variousness of hope.
He cannot know of spring's green slope
Or mountain woods where mild winds carry
Full-leafed and many-voiced directives,
And where his own sons will descend
To fertile, river-led perspectives.

NEAR OLYMPIC

West Los Angeles

The neighborhood, part Japanese and part
Chicano, wears its poverty like art
Exotic in its motley oddities.
Over dirt driveways hang banana trees;
In front of small square stucco houses bloom
Broad jacarandas whose rain-washed perfume
At morning half redeems the rush-hour released
Swelled roaring of the freeway six blocks east.
Along the street sit Fords and Oldsmobiles,
Lowslung and ancient, or—with raised rear wheels
And sides flame-painted—Mustangs and Chevelles.
And in the courtyards of one-time motels
In which the poorer families live, there grow
Sweet corn and yellow squash, and chickens go
Jerkily here and there, loud squawkings borne
Through limp, arched iris leaves and stalks of corn.

This, too, a neighborhood of nurseries
And of good gardeners. Walking by, one sees
Behind a block of chest-high chain-link fence,
In plastic round containers, succulents;
In small green boxes, blue forget-me-nots;
Ivies whose tendrils rise, staked, from glazed pots
In a sharp polish of small leafy claws;
Fresh hothouse orchids with their pelican jaws;
In tubs of earth, tangerine trees whose fruit
Hangs orangely pendulous, bright, and minute.
And ranged against the main garage's wall,
On shelves of blond boards and red bricks, are all
The bonsai: a one-foot, gold-wired pine,
Thick as a blacksmith's forearm, with a fine
Spray of huge needles; a squat, mossy oak,

Contorted as if by a thunderstroke;
A bougainvillaea massed with densities
Of pinkish blossoms and smooth, pointed leaves.
And over the front gate, a large sign says,
THE WORLD OF PLANTS—SUSHAWA AND MENDEZ,
The latter (a bandana handkerchief
Around his head) forever barking brief
Orders into an outdoor phone, burlesque
And confirmation of the picturesque.

Yet when at five the nursery Edens close,
Even the most naïve would not suppose
This place an Eden. Golden-dusked L.A.—
Bright flow of everywhere—goes its own way,
While here, convening in their curbside league,
Young men drink beer, a day of the fatigue
Of idleness behind them. Acid rock
Blasts from a nearby van, but sound can't shock
Those who've long heard it from their lethargy.
And in a yard with a dead pepper tree,
Some meager birds-of-paradise, and dirt,
A child grips balance at her mother's skirt.
A cat paws a toy soldier that it's found,
Prone at attention, on the width of ground
Running with cracks between the walk and street.
One of the young men rises to his feet,
Ready, and also ready not, to leave,
His Camels folded in his T-shirt's sleeve—
Carlos, chief dude of the rec center, slow
Hands in his pockets, mind on Mexico,
As the rich purple evening sky defines
A crescent moon above the power lines.

This is the hour of casual casualties.
Birds clatter in the stiff fronds of palm trees,
The bustle that the twilight's always fed.

The mother strokes her daughter's jet-black head;
The child makes choppy trooper steps toward the walk.
Some older children bike along the block,
A girl there crying, *No one catches me,*
Glancing back quickly, pumping furiously
Off from the others. Bent to handlebars,
Only one boy pursues her. Past parked cars,
It's *No one catches me,* and nearly night.
No eyes are following the girl's delight—
At least not Carlos's or the young mother's.
Nor do their eyes meet, ever, one another's.
It is as if they do not see or hear.
The mother will be nineteen come next year,
And Carlos twenty. What they are survives
The limpid vacancies of air, their lives
Now like some urgent, unobtrusive thing,
Withdrawn and lovely and diminishing.

NATIVE SYMPATHY

Perhaps it's wise to turn and hope to see
A welcoming expression on a face,
Though reason is a rare commodity,
Though courtesy is hardly commonplace.

For, if rebuffed, the senses still will solve
The fuzzy scent and surface of a peach.
Joys will return; a beachball will revolve
Breeze-prompted colors down a slope of beach.

A sober thought will rise, compelling rest,
Perhaps the thought of all those who've finessed
A little life from local circumstance,

Perhaps the memory (it, too, will do)
Of clouds whose whitely heaped extravagance
Held summer in a looming overview.

GOLDEN AGE

Even in fortunate times,
The nectar is spiked with woe.
Gods are incorrigibly
Capricious, and the needy
Beg in Nineveh or sleep
In paper-gusting plazas
Of the New World's shopping malls.

Meantime, the tyrant battens
On conquest, while advisers,
Angling for preferment, seek
Expedient paths. Heartbroken,
The faithful advocate looks
Back on cities of the plain
And trudges into exile.

And if any era thrives,
It's only because, somewhere,
In a plane tree's shade, friends sketch
The dust with theorems and proofs,
Or because, instinctively,
A man puts his arm around
The shoulder of grief and walks
It (for an hour or an age)
Through all its tears and telling.

THE WARTBURG, 1521–22

where Luther hides for ten months
after the Diet of Worms

The garden where he broods is like a riddle.
The circle of the gravel walk,
The sundial which is stationed in the middle,
A poppy on its hairy stalk:
These are like clues from which may be inferred
Imperatives of the Almighty's Word.

And nature veils, he thinks, a master plan.
Where hunters feel the woods grow level,
The hare the two dogs savage is frail Man,
The two dogs are the Pope and Devil;
And in the wind that courses through the forest,
He hears the pure truth the first angels chorused.

Odd, how his genius courts expectancy,
And views life as a text it's read.
Yet others, seeking God in all they see,
Not finding Him, will claim He's dead,
Or will descry false gods when history slips
Into a fraudulent Apocalypse.

This lies, however, centuries away.
The present prospect is of hills,
The garden which he walks in, day by day,
Leisure he restlessly fulfills,
While far below the fortress, the cascade
Drifts its cold white breath through the gorge's shade.

If everything's arranged, then even doubt
Is simply a predestined mood;
And thus he justifies, as he works out,

His theories and his solitude,
Gaining conviction while he frets and grieves
Till, one gray dawn in early March, he leaves.

Even this last scene's ambiguously spliced:
    The bridge creaks down, he rides across;
His mount's as humble as the mount of Christ;
    And, see, out there above the Schloss,
A widening band of chimney smoke is curled
Vaguely downwind, toward the modern world.

SHUCKING CORN

He plays the host, concerned with timing.
The guests, though, are the awkward sort:
Moths crashing on the screens and climbing
About in photophilic sport.

He sets the kettle on and tests
A casserole now nearly cooked;
She, on the porch's couch-swing, rests
And sees an ear they overlooked.

And then, the white silk gently torn,
She feeds a paper bag the husk.
He calls her; she holds up the corn,
As if a torch to light the dusk.

ON THE EVE OF A BIRTHDAY

As my Scotch, spared the water, blondly sloshes
About its tumbler, and gay manic flame
Is snapping in the fireplace, I grow youthful:
I realize that calendars aren't truthful
And that for all of my grand unsuccesses
External causes are to blame.

And if at present somewhat destitute,
I plan to alter, prove myself more able,
And suavely stroll into the coming years
As into rooms with thick rugs, chandeliers,
And colorfully pyramided fruit
On linened lengths of table.

At times I fear the future won't reward
My failures with sufficient compensation,
But dump me, aging, in a garret room
Appointed with twilit, slant-ceilinged gloom
And a lone bulb depending from a cord
Suggestive of self-strangulation.

Then, too, I have bad dreams, in one of which
A cowled, scythe-bearing figure beckons me.
Dark plains glow at his back; it seems I've died,
And my soul, weighed and judged, has qualified
For an extended, hyper-sultry hitch
Down in eternity.

Such fears and dreams, however, always pass.
And gazing from my window at the dark,
My drink in hand, I'm jauntily unbowed.
The sky's tiered, windy galleries stream with cloud,
And higher still, the dazed stars thickly mass
In their long Ptolemaic arc.

What constellated powers, unkind or kind,
Sway me, what far preposterous ghosts of air?
Whoever they are, whatever our connection,
I toast them (toasting also my reflection),
Not minding that the words which come to mind
Make the toast less toast than prayer:

Here's to the next year, to the best year yet;
To mixed joys, to my harum-scarum prime;
To auguries reliable and specious;
To times to come, such times being precious,
If only for the reason that they get
Shorter all the time.

NIGHTPIECE

Always the same voice
(And what voice pray tell?)
Sings me from sleep.

And when I tender the insomniac's complaints,
It points out the universe
Isn't sleeping, why should I
Expect more than this obscure interval
In which to read by this tensor light,
Stick-figured, jointed at the waist,
Its luminous, bowed head in an old-fashioned bonnet.

Strengthen the weak, cheer the downhearted,
Remember kindnesses received
Rather than injuries endured
(Always the same voice),
Forget not benefits,
Among which are numbered
Even these terrors of the dark.

How gigantic the dark,
How hopeful the litany.

THE LADY OF BRIGHT COUNSEL

". . . a discussion of Love that I heard from a Mantinean
woman named Diotima, who was wise in this and many
other matters."
PLATO, Symposium, 201D

It seems to her strange that the mind should observe
The very processes of which it's part.
And no less does a second thought unnerve:
Just when we get our bearings, we must start
To leave the much-in-little that enchants—
The two-way traffic of a file of ants,
The field of birds who chase, dive, or retire
To linear order on a span of wire.

Though doubtful, touching a responsive chord,
She sees beyond confusion after all.
By understating it, she's underscored
Her lesson: when the love we have will fall
To other women and to other men,
It will inspire us to life again.

SHORT SUBJECTS

for my sister Martha, who likes epigrams

1. SKULL AT THE CROSSROADS

   Disparage, if you will, the life you live:
   It's preferable to the alternative.

2. VOTARIES OF CUPID

   Together five minutes—and we're ashen
   With wrath and mutual disgust.
   Lovers should glow, love, with their passion,
   Not spontaneously combust.

3. APOLOGY

   You ask if you may see a sample
   Of what I'm working on—but, Ample,
   If I comply, then you feel free
   To shower your latest work on me,
   Petitioning evaluation.
   Though not of cynical persuasion,
   I feel your interest in my art
   Is that I'll take up, for my part,
   An interest in your own. To share
   One's labor is, I'm well aware,
   An act to which even gods descend.
   It is an act which I commend;
   It is an act which I can savor—
   But not when you return the favor.

4. YOUNG AMERICAN POETS HANDICAP

   All have his praise at the beginning.
   He watches us pound round the course,
   Happily assured of winning
   Because he's bet on every horse.

5. MATTHEW 5:15

Self-deprecating, you defer
In ways we're called on to admire:
Your lamp beneath a bushel, Sir,
Your object is to cause a fire.

6. SOCIAL REFORM

A prince of rational behavior,
Satan informs us that our Savior
Remarks we'll always have the poor,
Which moral saves expenditure.
We'll always have the poor? Okay.
Yet, looked at whole, the text will say
Something more lenitive, and truer.
We'll have the poor: let's make them fewer.

7. AN L.A. IMPROMPTU

Now this beau draws you, and that one estranges.
You're on and off romantic interchanges
With such gear-grinding, reflex-wrought decision
That it's a miracle there's no collision
Among the men who, over you and under,
Pursue you in a kind of heated wonder
Until you've stickshifted off and dismissed them.
You haven't a lovelife, you've a freeway system.

8. NATURAL HISTORY

He pours forth his fierce, quarrelsome twaddle;
If others speak, he's loath to hear.
Had men evolved along his model,
They'd have two mouths and but one ear.

9. At the Corner of the Counter of the Diner

Its size one trillionth of a proton,
This universe which theorists dote on
Burst out, it seems, in THE BIG BANG.
As if a sort of boomerang,
The whole affair—its stars and spaces,
Its quasars, quarks, and eating places—
May one day seek to reassume
The compact quarters of its womb
And may by violent recensions
Collapse back to its first dimensions.
This would, it seems, be THE BIG CRUNCH,
The merest thought of which spoils lunch.

10. Mirror for Morning

My razor's harvested its foam.
One hand, like upward calipers,
Measures my chin, and, like a comb,
The other rumplingly confers
Some order on my rebel locks.
A face a mother could resist?
Yes, and a source of paradox,
Fertile (down to his very socks)
Material for the satirist.

11. Family Album

I turn a page. At once, breathtakingly,
You hold me sadly, steadily, in view.
Is it because you can't return to me,
Or is it that I'm journeying to you?

Last Tango

It is disquieting, that film
In which the plagued protagonist
Won't tell his lover who he is.
It's not just that she turns on him
Or that his youth and age consist
Primarily of chances missed:
The most disturbing thing's that he,
Who loses all else, cannot lose
His own identity.

All life conspires to define us,
Weighing us down with who we are,
Too much drab pain. It is enough
To make one take sides with Plotinus:
Sweet Universal Avatar,
Make me pure spirit, an ensouled star—
Or something slightly less divine:
Rain on an awning, or wind rough
Among clothes on a line.

Of course, it wouldn't do to flee
All longings, griefs, despairs, and such.
Blisses anonymously pursued
Destroy us or, evasively,
Both yield to and resist our touch.
The Brando figure learns as much:
A wholly personal collapse
Succeeds his nameless interlude.
One thinks, though, that perhaps

In some less fallen world, an ease
Might grace our necessary fictions.
There, our identities would be
Like—what?—like Haydn's symphonies,

Structures of balanced contradictions,
For all their evident restrictions,
Crazy with lightness and desire:
La Passione, Mercury,
Tempesta, Mourning, Fire.

IN THE KING'S ROOMS

David, at Mahanaim during the Rebellion

This evening I pace chambers where I sought
To charm an old king with a shepherd's song.
Now I am king, and aging. I once thought
I could forever dwell in quiet caught
From melodies I crafted. I was wrong.

Young, loved by all, I lived beyond all doubt.
I calmed the trembling flank and frightened eye
Of the young doe—and later, led the rout
Of the invaders, lifting with a shout
The giant's head up to an answering sky.

Despised now even by my son, I raise
No shout to heaven. An uncertain friend,
A faithless leader, I can only gaze
Across a land which lent me, once, its praise
And which tonight I grudgingly defend.

Let my smooth, artful counselors secure
Victories in the name of faith and truth.
I can no longer care. Nor am I sure
Whom I should pray forgiveness for—
The old man misled or the too-favored youth.

TIMOTHY

Although the field lay cut in swaths,
Grass at the edge survived the crop:
Stiff stems, with lateral blades of leaf,
Dense cattail flower-spikes at the top.

If there was breeze and open sky,
We raked each swath into a row;
If not, we took the hay to dry
To the barn's golden-showering mow.

The hay we forked there from the truck
Was thatched resilience where it fell,
And I took pleasure in the thought
The fresh hay's name was mine as well.

Work was a soothing, rhythmic ache;
Hay stuck where skin or clothes were damp.
At length, the pickup truck would shake
Its last stack up the barn's wood ramp.

Pumping a handpump's iron arm,
I washed myself as best I could,
Then watched the acres of the farm
Draw lengthening shadows from the wood

Across the grass, which seemed a thing
In which the lonely and concealed
Had risen from its sorrowing
And flourished in the open field.

CHANSON PHILOSOPHIQUE

The nominalist in me invents
A life devoid of precedents.
The realist takes a different view:
He claims that all I feel and do
Billions of others felt and did
In history's Pre-me period.

Arguing thus, both voices speak
A partial truth. I am unique,
Yet the unceasing self-distress
Of desire buffets me no less
Than it has other sons of man
Who've come and gone since time began.

The meaning, then, of this dispute?
My life's a nominal/real pursuit,
Which leaves identity clear and blurred,
In which what happens has occurred
Often and never—which is to say,
Never to me, or quite this way.

THE TREATISE ON HARMONY

School out, children come through the gate,
Behind them the playground's pavement
With its painted circles and squares,
Its intersections of pastimes.
Boys whistle and call, two dueling
With imaginary swords, thrust
And parry, one advancing, one
Backing, while a girl at the curb

Cranes to see Is the bus coming,
And another, serious in
Blue-bowed pigtails and sailor's blouse,
Leads a younger friend by the hand.
At the children's approach, sparrows
Foraging the walk spurt up to
And through the lozenges of space
Formed by links of the playground fence,

And trees crisply shake themselves, leaves
And the voices beneath them like,
Almost, an orchestra tuning,
Woodwinds, violins, the courtly
Emphasis of a kettledrum,
Confused sound promising music
Expressive of youth, contentious
Or firmly ordered, glad and grave.

JACARANDA

for Sumiye and Dick Kobashigawa

Higher than the camellia trees,
Among whose leaves pine needles land,
The jacaranda's ferns are fanned
In the yard's docile resident breeze.

I read and watch in shifting light.
A small bug, purposeful, unwary,
Explores a page's printed prairie
And, as I turn it, takes to flight.

Impatiens, modestly profuse,
Bloom by a fence, along whose boards,
Wedge-pointed, a squirrel deftly fords
A child's slant M's and W's.

And at a lattice of bamboo,
With trailing strings of bleeding hearts,
A hummingbird appears, hangs, darts,
Sinks, and then vanishes from view.

I see, too, on a phone line, rock
Some doves whose converse is so sweet,
You'd think harsh words passed through their feet
Might be transformed to gentler talk.

And its trunk buttressed by a pole,
The pepper tree stirs its willowy boughs,
Among which hangs a little house,
Its door a peg and a round hole.

Here a plump short-billed finch returns.
He perches to survey the yard

With his quick eye, and to regard,
It seems, the jacaranda's ferns,

Which can't be otherwise construed
Than lowly beauty raised aloft,
Limberly bowed about and soft,
To a befitting altitude.

An Aubade

As she is showering, I wake to see
A shine of earrings on the bedside stand,
A single yellow sheet which, over me,
Has folds as intricate as drapery
In paintings from some fine old master's hand.

The pillow which, in dozing, I embraced
Retains the salty sweetness of her skin;
I sense her smooth back, buttocks, belly, waist,
The leggy warmth which spread and gently laced
Around my legs and loins, and drew me in.

I stretch and curl about a bit and hear her
Singing among the water's hiss and race.
Gradually the early light makes clearer
The perfume bottles by the dresser's mirror,
The silver flashlight, standing on its face,

Which shares the corner of the dresser with
An ivy spilling tendrils from a cup.
And so content am I, I can forgive
Pleasure for being brief and fugitive.
I'll stretch some more, but postpone getting up

Until she finishes her shower and dries
(Now this and now that foot placed on a chair)
Her fine-boned ankles, and her calves and thighs,
The pink full nipples of her breasts, and ties
Her towel up, turban-style, about her hair.

SUMMER

Voluptuous in plenty, summer is
Neglectful of the earnest ones who've sought her.
She best resides with what she images:
Lakes windless with profound sun-shafted water;
Dense orchards in which high-grassed heat grows thick;
The one-lane country road where, on his knees,
A boy initials soft tar with a stick;
Slow creeks which bear flecked light through depths of trees.

And he alone is summer's who relents
In his poor enterprisings; who can sense,
In alleys petal-blown, the wealth of chance;
Or can, supine in a deep meadow, pass
Warm hours beneath a moving sky's expanse,
Chewing the sweetness from long stalks of grass.

WAITING FOR THE STORM

Breeze sent a wrinkling darkness
Across the bay. I knelt
Beneath an upturned boat,
And, moment by moment, felt

The sand at my feet grow colder,
The damp air chill and spread.
Then the first raindrops sounded
On the hull above my head.

At Will Rogers Beach

1

Among the swells, the storm past, surfers sit,
 Lifting and sinking in and out of view.
On the horizon, ranged clouds counterfeit
 An Orient Alps; sunlight plunges through
Loose standing billows, and the waves' swift wash
Shoots in with bubblingly confused panache,
 Encircling, as it seethes, a melting fort
 Topped with cup-molded turrets of dark sand,
 While small sandpipers zigzag in a sort
 Of shoulder-hunched brigade along the strand.

2

The aisle of autumn sunlight settling on
 The mobile corrugations of the sea
Fragments and forms at once, is here and gone,
 A durable, elusive energy:
Pure presence and repose—mere lovely being
To feel which is as natural as seeing
 The dog that dashes up the beach and back
 Or, to a pair of onlookers' applause,
 Goes skidding to a posture of attack
 And leaps to snatch a Frisbee in his jaws.

3

A man wades with a fishing rod and pail
 Across the soft sand, over which a kite
Makes snapping loops as it pursues its tail.
 One notes gulls weaving at a breezy height
And the lithe power of the tide's advance,

But notes as well the berm's small jousting lance
    (A plastic drink top run through with a straw),
        The fissure where the berm's sand crust has cracked,
    And shingle pebbles which, when waves withdraw,
        Perform their clattering, scraping tumbling act.

4

The wind dies, and the cloud Alps disappear,
    And where the sun now sets, the sky's so swirled
With smoky colors that the atmosphere
    Seems like the abstract beauty of the world.
The swells more regular, there floats at rest
A pelican, long beak tucked to its chest.
    Holding torpedo-shaped red rescue buoys,
        Two lifeguards chat, as surfers, one by one,
    Stagger in through the shallows' mist and noise
        Or paddle back out for a final run.

5

What this abundance means, one cannot say.
    One merely wants to shelter it from harm;
One merely sees the waves burst into spray
    Out where the jetty casts its bouldered arm;
One merely feels the heart contract that this
Should all be utterly precarious.
    It's nearly dark, but there's still light enough
        For those—the surfers' landward counterparts—
    Who roller-skate the walk below the bluff,
        Rehearsing their adroit, spontaneous arts.

6

One of them coasts upright, visoring a hand
    To the sun's afterglow, while, smooth performers,
Two others click past a closed hot-dog stand,
    She in a T-shirt, shorts, tights, and leg warmers,
He in light gym trunks and a netted top;
And where the long wide pavement curves, they drop
    Into a slight crouch and accelerate,
        Cross-stepping, their arms swinging left and right,
    Translating into speed their form and weight
      And dwindling, as they sweep off, into night.

THE CHORUS

Because fate thought us minor, we stood back
While others took their cues on center stage.
We saw them, trembling, spring to an attack
We knew would fail. Then, desperate to assuage
Their horrors when despair supplanted rage,
    We somehow steadied them in the belief
    There was a higher purpose in their grief.

We saw and felt their passions. We can tell
Of Philoctetes' suppurating wound;
Of how horse-taming Hector stood and fell,
As on the wall old Priam howled and swooned;
Of Palamedes, beaten to the ground
    And stoned with those same tablets, smooth and white,
    With which he had taught men to count and write.

We couldn't save them, and if we wore masks,
It was to hide the bitterest of tears.
To the sensation-seeking voice which asks
For tales of tumult, flashing shields and spears,
We have no answer, standing in arrears
    To those who could not take the paths we urged,
    But met their terrors head on, and were purged.

This friend, that lover, dear comrades-in-arms:
They hold all meaning we were meant to know.
We've closed their eyes the last time. Safe from harms,
They follow courses where the planets go,
And we who live are solaced, for although
    The years have plundered us of strength and youth,
    We served the gods' commands. We spoke the truth.

But Home Is Here

April has returned
Box scores to the papers,
Scrub jays to the lawn

(How they bounce!—feet forward
Like long-jumpers landing),
And I fix dinner for one.

My arm raised, the egg cracked,
The quick rope of the white
Lowers yoke to mixing bowl,

A seeded hemisphere
Of sliced tomato
Rocking on the cutting board.

The days growing longer,
I sing to the trees,
The flowering pear and persimmon,

To the morning glories
Which insinuate vines
Through knotholes in the fence:

Life, life, how sad, how rushed
You are, how self-divided,
Cells doubling and parting

Into patterns and flows,
To complication,
To oblivion.

When the cat arches
On my leg, I sweep her up
And hold her above me, pleading,

Calypso, make me not
Immortal but happy
On earth: send me home.

Ah, but home is here.
With a salad and omelette,
And the darkness coming

Like a friend, like the hope
Of wisdom arriving,
However late.

ANGEL

At Christmas season, when the tree was trimmed,
I'd lie beneath a ceiling veined and limbed
And splashed with color from the blinking lights.
Not far below the treetop's five-bulb star,
An angel cruised the decorated heights,
Playing a papier-mâché guitar.

I'd hear my brother's crackling radio
And sense the privacy of night and snow.
The living room itself was rearranged
To make way for the tree, sofas and chairs
Moved back against the wall, their aspect changed
By occupying space not usually theirs.

All through that altered Advent atmosphere,
The angel played a strain I couldn't hear,
Perhaps no less melodious for the fact.
The colors soothed, the darkened room was warm;
The angel, if inscrutably abstract,
Appeared designed to hearten and inform.

Sometimes I'd climb a chair and take it down.
It had a flowing, multifolded gown,
A wave of hair arrested by a wing,
But though its smile comprised a pursed mild line,
Whichever way I turned it on its string,
Its eyes looked elsewhere, never meeting mine.

LOVE POEM

for Victoria

The story's told of speechless Pierrot's
Defense of his secluded tower.
Beleaguered by imaginary foes,
Relying simply on his anxious power,
He would toil up the stairway every night,
Then rush round madly when the moon arose
To drive away the moon's invasive light.

The clutched-at beams always escaped his grasp
Effortlessly. Distracted wraith!
His hands had nothing but themselves to clasp;
Mute self-absorption was his only faith.
Brave as he was, frustration made him weep,
And balked by force elusive as his breath,
He sank at last into exhausted sleep.

If, like poor Pierrot, I've anxiously
Dwelt in my life, the spell is broken.
Awakened to your touch and voice, I see
That evil is the formless and unspoken,
And that peace rests in form and nomenclature,
Which render our two natures—formerly
Discomfited, self-conscious—second nature.

THE SKIMMING STONE

in memory of Billy Knight,
who died of a heart attack, age 38

The factory on the river, during lunch
We'd skim stones to a current brown and slow.
The shore was pebbles that our boots would scrunch
As we searched back and forth for stones to throw.
Most of the stones were poor New England slate;
A few had—smooth and round—the proper weight,
And we'd spin off long runs and argue whether
To count concluding skips that merged together.

Once when the whistle called us from the shore,
You pocketed a stone. Was it for luck?
Or did you feel a specially close rapport
That day with life, with youth? Or were you struck
Merely that the stone's smooth warmth implied
A longer rather than a shorter ride?

Toward Calgary

Out over these parched, gusty plains,
Loose dirt is lifted to a sail;
Beyond wide distances, a train's
Smoke draws a horizontal trail.

Posts bear a wire, mile after mile,
Across deep views toward which winds roll,
That wire the only obstacle
Between the winds and the North Pole.

Here one could drive what seems an age,
Seeing no more than leveled land
And, on the road, slow-skidding sage
And skating shapes of windblown sand.

Here one could try the radio's dial
And, as the inching needle slips
Through far, infrequent static, feel
A stilled world at the fingertips.

And one might sense nothing but thirst
Or soundless hours in this place
Where all horizons are dispersed
Continuously into space.

Yet from caked, crumbly ground and rocks
The spiky purple lupines grow
And cacti shaped like tuning forks.
And some who've crossed such precincts know

The prudent heart is like these plains,
Where quietness has grown immense,
No landmarks rendering its terrains
Measurable to human sense,

And where, remote of any tree,
The sky is an inclusive drift
Of radiance chastening, endlessly,
Needless invention, needless thrift.

Uncertainties
and Rest

1979

For Brad and Martha

WITH A COPY OF RONALD FIRBANK

So much for dreaming. Light winds still distress
The fragrant shrubs and elegant parterre,
But in the palace court, His Weariness
The Prince is just a presence on the air.

Nor are the cellars filled with Grand Marnier.
And gone, alas, the celebrated guests:
Carmen Étoile, Pirelli, the coryphée,
The daughter of the famous flagellists.

In the obscurity, such innocence.
"What every soldier knows is understood."
Tag-ends of belief, dialogue, stock scenes—
Yet the books were, however minor, good.

Good but neglected. Or was that a part
Of the design? Even the Queen could see
That fame may prove "très gutter" and that art
Is often just pretentious fantasy.

And though the mannerisms seem somewhat thin,
The kingdoms, in decline, are always there.
And even if they weren't, the novelist
Would understand. Or simply wouldn't care.

SUNDAY AFTERNOON

adapting a line from Alexander Barclay

"Winter is near and the world is too hard."
And the phone, one might add, is disconnected.
In the tame isolation of my yard
I rake the last leaves. To be respected

And loved made sense to me once, but of late
I'm drawn by more workable conceits;
And the stiff, rooftop antics of a kite
And the leisure of broad, deserted streets

Seem to outweigh the needs of sentiment.
The clouds shift, the light alters, and I pass
Serenely through the afternoon, intent
On nothing but the leaves and the dead grass.

So calm, so settled. Such peace is the best.
And sheltered in the remnants of the day,
I gather what I want, and leave the rest
To the vague sounds of traffic, far away.

PROFILS PERDUS

for T.R. "For him, only the evanescent existed; no
substance, no tradition; just a spirit of travel,
the moment."

It does not matter if in Rome that fall
You, leaning on the rail of the balcony,
Watched a young woman pace the yard below,
Her parasol
Now raised, now shouldered. Nor need you feel, see,

More in the sudden rain which, in Marseilles,
Forced you into that church than the stained glass,
Or the four white candles, or the vast stillness,
Or the way
The marble echoes rippled through the Mass.

Nostalgia is your last, your perfect, fate.
In the vague wash of circumstance, you know
That any instant can in you assume
All the weight
And feeling of the absolute. And so,

What matters, simply, is that you contain
Both past and future; that sometime, somewhere,
You will yourself become the moment—an
Indefinite rain,
A profile disappearing in the air.

Stargazing at Barton

For the child who leans out over
the sill, mindful of the curtains,
may these stars be names remembered:
Taurus, Orion, and The Bear—
tranquil distances and moon-hung
bazaars the gods once frequented.

When Pascal speaks of "nothingness
from which we're drawn, infinity
in which we're swallowed up," he does
not mean this mid-August sky, this
quiet of meadows that has the
power to calm us. The alder

in the yard rattles in the wind;
and, from the woods, the rumble and
rush of a brook. Surely, we live
and care how we live. Undimin-
ished by our old contemplation,
the starlight remains fugitive

and beautiful, if only for
the child who loves it as it is,
who sees, leaning across the sill,
Taurus, Orion, and The Bear,
masters of their ancient distance,
bright and fading, immutable.

SUBURBS OF THE SEA

I. EVENING, AFTER THE AUCTION

Now nothing on the lawn but a cane chair
Of dubious value, and a paper cup
Capsized by the rose bush. The auctioneer
Stands on the sagging front steps, adding up

The profits for the late Miss Randel's heir.
The dead survive in trust and metaphors,
And she'd no doubt be proud to see what care
Went into this, how much that chest of drawers

Cost in the public dusk. The past, for hire,
Is still the past—though with a paradox:
In time, the worthless and the old acquire
Commercial dignity. The elm-lined walks

Flatter the secondhand and the beautiful,
As the auctioneer knows. If there is no mark
Of better times, at least the air is cool
And the lawn empty as the sky grows dark.

II. HISTORY OF A FRIENDSHIP IN MATTAPOISETT

It starts with sherry and an armchair cruise.
        Then, nights in front of the fire screen;
Sap bubbling from the logs, there's coffee and
        The comforts of occasional news—
The wedding of a friend, books read, films seen.

Formality is a renewable disguise,
        Well-worded distance. Fog rolls in;
The tide turns. In this suburb of the sea,
        We do not overanalyze;
        We take on faith what we have been.

This morning, in your absence, scratch pads fill
  With curlicue and arabesque.
Slowly, appropriately, the fire sinks;
  Dust gathers on the window sill;
  And I clear papers from my desk,

My thoughts my own as rain drips from the eaves.
  Tact is at once acquired and shed:
In ending or beginning, it is natural
  To ask for certain clarities.
But something, always, must be left unsaid.

III. A COUPLE, A DOMESTIC INTERIOR

on a photograph with the inscription: Vermont, 1903

Everything's focused: the globe lamps declare
a rolltop desk and bookcase; the grained air
is still. She is sewing; he looks on,
mustached and casual—though he clearly knows
that at any moment the shutter will close.

She appears somewhat cautious, too, but why?
Nothing's out of place. Curled on the floor,
their setter; and on the far wall, his portrait
and two oval mirrors that amplify
the harmony and light. Or is there more?

A mistress in Sherbrooke? a land deal he
pulled off to pay a gambling debt?
And on her side—a son who hates her? the
persistent fear of growing old alone?
a lover from her youth she can't forget?

Or is it merely that there's something tense
and forced about their innocence,
a willed denial of living? Still,

they look so solid, as if they knew
they'd only have to hold their pose until

the camera flashed once—and then they'd be
not simply granted security,
but fixed forever in the quiet here:
a man, a woman, a long afternoon,
calm, domestic, perfectly clear.

IV. SUMMER FAIRYTALE

It's once upon a thirty-first of June,
    A small man spinning flax to gold;
And we beguile the minor afternoon
Amid a wilderness of hollyhocks,
    While, elsewhere, princes climb to old
Disasters via fair Rapunzel's locks.

We find our peace in evenings of croquet,
    The thought of Gretel in her clearing;
Yet when the late sun glitters on the bay,
And overhead the seagulls wheel and pass,
    We grow abstracted, barely hearing
The click of ball and mallet on the grass.

Even a fruitful magic by degrees
    Can wrap us in a dubious spell;
Tales that articulated mysteries
Now offer only ways of looking back,
    As though across the ocean's swell,
Or down alleys through the pine and tamarack.

Though legends of no very different stripe
    Will help, we hope, our children see
Themselves as symbol or as archetype
As well as what their private fates devise,
    We mistrust fictive sorcery
And wish our past and aging otherwise.

57

THE MESSENGER

Of you, messenger, we ask only
Some intelligence of the weather
Or crops, or word from relatives in
The next village. These mornings, thin smoke

Rises from the chimney of the house
Across the valley. Late asters bloom
By forest pools black with reflected firs,
And never have our lives been so rich.

Do not then bring us tidings of wars
To the north, frozen rivers, passes
Blocked with snow. Enough that, certain nights,
We hear the osier clicking in wind

And sense all catastrophes you bear;
Enough that once we gave a stranger
Confidences of a nature that
Wiser men would never commit to

Another's keeping. We recognize
Shadow where it falls. Yet, messenger,
Know when you come that we will greet you
With all suitable formality;

Know that for you our table is laid,
The dark wine broached. Grow warm at our fire
And, when you are ready to, speak. We,
Bearers of other lives, will listen.

Incident on a Picnic

At length we tired of arguing, and drank
What little wine was left.
I leaned back on a bank
Of clover, and still thinking deft

Ripostes to what you'd said,
I noticed by the field below
A girl of ten or so
Who leaned across the pasture bar and fed

A calf a handful of grass.
You saw her too—and (I could see)
Felt the same shame that ran through me.
Did our self-serving angers pass

From us that moment? I can't say,
But I know that walking home that day
We weren't too certain or too proud
To note the roadside scent of hay

And the sky's white ribs of cloud.

LEARNING TO SKATE

for Pam Newton

Back on the beach, your uncle's Irish setter
    Gallops, ears flapping, through the snow;
    I clutch a handful of your sweater
And half-contriving balance, let you tow

Me to the wide mouth of the bay. We sight
    Buoys frozen in their tilt and torque,
    Ice-fishing huts, a streak of white
In the sky above the mountains of New York.

Arms swinging easily, you pick up speed.
    Blue-black depths gliding under us,
    I let go and coast swiftly, freed
To rapture gathered from your impetus.

Returned to shore, I lean against a boulder;
    Hunched over, you unlace your skates.
    And there (above, beyond, your shoulder)
A young girl is rehearsing figure-8's

One after another, her long red scarf streaming,
    Three, five, seven—ten or more!
    I'll do that, too, I think, day-dreaming
In January, 1954.

For My Mother

Barton, Vermont

It was late August. Standing by the well,
I watched you gather wildflowers in the brake.
Red clover, goldenrod, and chamomile,
The dragonflies and sunlight in the air—
And you waist-deep in all that color there.
So young, you seemed then. There was hay to make

And a cloud shadow on the Stevens' hill.
We two had grown apart, but I could see,
That moment, what you once were, and are still.
Only the light could touch you. The divorce,
Your father's death, the hard years: these, of course,
Were there, too. But your curiosity

And quiet were as wild as weeds, set off
From all the past. Mother, I know your ways:
Columbian prints; the mild defensive cough
You fill a silence with; that picnic ease,
Talk, and a paper plate poised on your knees.
Yet I was startled. Innocent of days,

How much of pain and learning we survive!
And I, discovering what I'd known before,
Stood silent in your calm, the light alive
And perfect as you finished your bouquet,
The wind and the long grass rippling away.
Nor did I call you. Nor could I ask more.

An Interlude of Epigrams

1.

Here lies Sir Tact, a diplomatic fellow
Whose silence was not golden, but just yellow.

2. Beethoven's Ninth at the Hollywood Bowl

The chorus sings, musicians play,
But on a stage so far away,
It is as if we strain to hear
The 1824 premiere.

3.

You asked me in to dine, and now just talk
Of Hegel, Mozart, a Picasso nude.
Your learning's splendid, but it's ten o'clock—
You've lots of food for thought, now where's the food?

4. Pal

When we're together you invariably ask
Advice and consolation. I don the mask
Of sympathy, lips pursed as you run through
Tales of misfiring conquests, a snafu
Involving an irate Ms. and a Mrs.
Who teaches yoga. What a sad world this is!
So difficult, so fraught with complication!
Concluding, you express appreciation:
So kind of you to always hear me out,
I need a friend, a true friend. Well, no doubt,
Yet if I ever speak to you in kind, you
Grow nervous, tense; my problems just remind you
Of meetings that you're late for. *So distressing*
Your situation, yes, but I've this pressing
Engagement. . . . Fair enough. But you should know

I've wearied of this curious quid pro quo.
You talk, I listen; when I talk, you flee—
And I'm afraid, though it much troubles me,
I'd best forego the joys of our relations
Henceforth. As for your future lamentations,
One listener should prove as good as another.
It's not a friend you need, friend, but a mother.

5. ELEGY FOR A FIRST NOVEL

Small book, that struggled to withstand
The flourish of my eager hand,
Forgive the plotless, fatal welter
Of the youth I tried to shelter.

6. HISTORY OF MORALS, OR *THE OLD CURIOSITY SHOP*

While granddad gambles, the plot thickens;
Nell shields and serves him faithfully,
And what seems innocence to Dickens
To us seems codependency.

7. MILLENNIAL VISIONS

Mankind goes bonkers, but a day will dawn
When we'll lay down our weapons and our cars.
People will live in peace and condos on
A terraformed and habitable Mars,
And arts foundations will distribute grants
To talented and worthy applicants.

8. A MILLION LAUGHS

No one can out-lampoon, -joke, -quip, or -pun you,
But the funnier you get the more we shun you.
The moral, sir? He who possesses wit
Should also have the sense to ration it.

9.

No human fault is lost on Fuss,
And he can dissect each of us
Neatly in terms of his own choosing,
Sly, irritated, or amusing.
You wonder who escapes critique?
Who in our circle's spared his pique?
Whom he approves of? None of us
Unless, of course, you're counting Fuss.

10. *SUNT BONA, SUNT QUAEDAM MEDIOCRIA . . .*

Martial, you're right. Even the best collection
Of poetry will prove, upon inspection,
A volume all too slender and too piddling
With some good poems, some bad, some fair to middling.

FAMILY REUNION

It is a country life. For supper, rice
And meatloaf. The blue china plates suggest
The past. Nostalgia, quiet and precise,
Is all we ask for and desire here:
At such reunions, mere discretion's best.
We eat, we talk, and afterwards we clear

The table off for a few hours of bridge.
Over coffee, we bid hand after hand
As the sun sinks behind a birch-lined ridge.
Four clubs and double—and each card is led
Within the ease of conversation and
The resonance of what is never said.

Tonight good nature's served up family-style.
The children's problems, the insurance bills,
Are indexed in another place. And while
There is no real change, everything will yield,
At least for now, to vistas of blue hills,
Or the silence of a still and dripping field.

And it's a resolution of sorts. Staid,
Together for the past, if nothing more,
We share the same relaxing masquerade—
A life that's always gentle, never strict,
In which there's space enough for us and for
Lies we no longer care to contradict.

Coda in Wind

Now moonlight has defined
The agile spruce and fir,
And though we draw the blind
We hear their dark limbs stir

The mild, familiar air
That we would shut outside
If only we knew where,
Or when, or what, to hide.

THIS IS

This is a child's forest: moss
and stunted pine, the bell-flowered
arbutus. In the predawn dark,
lichen glows on the tree trunks,

and then, among the trees, smoky
light, the white wreathings of our breath
on the cold air. No rider passes,
no hooves recall the earth,

and yet I remember that in such a place
I crossed a frozen stream
and saw, through the clear ice,
dark trout, green weeds.

That silence was of the mind.
But now, far away, bees are swarming;
drunk with noon, they cluster
in the mouths of enormous blossoms;

and here, before us, the fern's shadow
quivers; pollen fills the air. Be
calm. Going, we make no sound.
Our feet do not feel the earth.

Three Notes toward Definitions

I. Of Culture

Culture. It's an ingredient used in making
Pineapple yogurt, Gothic cathedrals.
It's Isaac Newton's experiments with prisms—
Its opposite being, one supposes,
Fried chicken TV dinners, plastic roses,
Confessional novels brimming over
With soul and solecisms.

One also should record how closely it
And water are related. Tiber<->Rome,
Greece<->the Aegean, Dr. Johnson<->tea.
One might additionally note
That it involves things beautiful (e.g.,
Fine thread, clear glass, a Mozart serenade,
A brooch of amethyst or jade).

Druids observing this or that eclipse
Surely possess it. So does Socrates,
Who calmly lifts the hemlock to his lips.
And those firm, savagely aware
New England matrons have it in their way,
As do Ben Franklin, Billie Holliday,
Shakespeare, and Fred Astaire.

That none of this recalls M. Arnold's phrase
About pursuing light and sweetness
Should not concern us. The soul seeks completeness,
And throughout the bewilderments it's dealt,
The spirit seeks its proper scope.
Culture? It's life humanely felt.
(See too Politeness, Mercy, Hope.)

II. OF FAITH

A puzzling topic, this. Should be filed under
Assurance, Things Unseen, Intimations. Yet
For all of its obscurities, it is
Expressed innumerably in objects—viz.,
A pencil, a French cigarette,
Suspension bridges, drawings of the sea,
Etchings of Japanese severity.

Which is to say that all of the above
(Pardon, dear reader, the didactic vein)
Imply convictions that our lives sustain.
Despite newspapers, bills, the efforts of
The politician, *Something real exists:*
And we in turn, by faith, produce
A further something for delight or use.

Granted, too smooth a formulation,
But it suggests a certain truth:
It is the incomplete and unexplored
That often offer the most true reward.
(See Hebrews 11:1–33,
St. Augustine's *Confessions,* Pascal's *Pensées,*
Darwin's *Autobiography.*)

So, too, by faith one may be led
To recognitions of a wealth of splendors:
The fine blond down on a child's wrist,
A dark field sheltered by an arm of mist,
The puddle in the driveway which reflects
A network of bare branches overhead.
Which brings us to the point that faith respects

Even the values of a fallen world.
Rimbaud discovered love in the bizarre,
Duccio an opulence in the austere.

So may we, in inauspicious weather
Or inauspicious labor, be aware
Of an angelic gift—though angels are
Another matter altogether.

III. OF FRIENDSHIP

Byron considered it *love without wings.*
Others associate it with long views
Of hills and lakes. Still others tend to muse
Upon the darker side of things:
Stale beer, unanswered letters, or a pal
All too Shakespearean. (Cross references:
Iago, Enobarbus, Brutus, Hal.)

The standard modifiers aren't, alas,
Illuminating. "Steadfast," "warm," and "feeling"
Don't indicate the strength we need in dealing
With someone else's longings and regrets.
True friendship never is serene.
(Madame de Sévigné? Proust? Seymour Glass?)
Misunderstandings, vagaries of spleen,

All the minutiae of despair—
It is in spite of these one comes to share
Experience, and sharing it, confirms
The Other in The Other's terms
And not one's own. (Consult as well Restriction,
Patience, and Love.) Though life may be construed
As merely a Cartesian fiction,

We yet respond to its detail:
A morning by the ocean, the horizon
Asserted by a single sail;
The neighbor's Siamese; a fireside talk
(Preferably with evening come)

Embellished by refreshments which recall
The wines in Plato's *Symposium*.

Or putting matters in another way,
We might (again invoking Johnson) say
That friendship offers troubles we're inclined
To cherish. Solitude is bliss?
There's that opinion, to be sure.
But there are ills of heart and mind
Which only companionship can cure.

AUTOBIOGRAPHY

It has, after all, certain advantages.
When one writes about oneself, one is always
Careful to do justice to the subject. Then,
Too, there's room for digression: "He was, perhaps,
More obscure than sublime," "It was a privilege
To witness such confusion," and "A saint should
Never be too obvious." Vanity is
Condoned. As the master resembles his dog,
The writer resembles his book.
                              Consider.
The most thorough biographer is obliged
To distort. His history authenticates
Only itself; the life must fit the design.
Though the real figure may be no more honest,
There is this difference: he and the reader are
Equally deceived, and his own words prescribe
The deception. Or, as a philosopher
Once remarked, "True glass, however cracked or flawed,
Will admit light." The moral being, of course,
That integrity is inescapable.

DON JUAN: A WINTER CONVALESCENCE

Agreed: the orange juice lacked finesse,
Bouquet, and character. He drank it, though;
It offered reassurance, more or less,
A sense of well-being as he settled back
Underneath several layers of calico
　　With last year's *Farmer's Almanack*.

Each evening, he would gaze across
The garden: bare-vined arbor, row of spruce,
A fountain filled with ice, two urns whose moss
Was dusted with fresh snow, a weathervane,
And that forbidding statue. Not Cockaigne,
　　But it consoled him—like the juice,

The warm quilts, or some turn of phrase
From an old journal. Lint on his lapel,
The doctor diagnosed his malady
As *something which would pass in a few days*.
(Was *something* influenza, or ennui?)
　　Regardless, he would soon be well,

And since he had nothing left to share
Except the dull dreams of the unconfessed
He could, in flawless self-immurement, stare
Out at the garden and that perfect row
Of spruce trees, and that statue, and that snow—
　　Claiming there much more than he guessed.

Nightpiece for the Summer Solstice

The guests gone, I stack up the paper plates.
The folding chairs no longer look unstable;
A swarm of midges clusters and dilates
Over the picnic table;

And I recall, *In country meadows, mists*
Are starting their white conquest of the land—
Lines written when I thought French Symbolists
Were part of a brass band.

The soul may suffer a fastidious twitch,
And yet such schoolboy verse seems fitting now,
This mothy, lilac evening being more rich
Than good taste might allow.

Sounds of a neighbor's lawnmower, the elms
Unstirring in full leaf, the squirrel that lopes
Over the dark grass seem of other realms,
Dream worlds in which all hopes

Are granted a sufficiency of light.
What stars define the sky now day is finished,
Define it of a world which, though in night,
Is green and undiminished.

STRICTLY ROMANTIC: COASTAL TOWN IN MAINE

Wave after wave explodes and flings
Up through the rocks, and then
In tentacle-like slitherings
Drains back. "The graves of men

Who came before us were such seas."
Just so. And in the haze
Of August, light shifts with the breeze,
And these seem merely days,

Miraculous and utterly
Unnecessary. Here,
The bells of Angelus will be
A voice; the sails that clear

The harbor will complete the sky.
This is the summer's course,
The natural becoming by
Returning to its source,

Its presence always on the edge
Of endless afternoons,
Wind in the eelgrass and salt sedge,
Wildflowers in the dunes.

AT THE SUMMIT

It was the wind, perhaps,
Snapping at my sleeve
That made it seem unreal.
By then the air had grown
So thin it hurt to breathe;
The sound of trees would rise,
And gather, and collapse
About us where we stood.
Below us lay the gorge—
White water and dark wood.

It was so close to ease,
That day: we had enough
Of openness and space.
In time the forest's sough
Died down, and we, descending,
Found poppies, a deer's track—
And all of it unreal,
Even looking back.

BAKER BEACH AT SUNSET

July 4, 1976

This is a place the ocean comes to die,
A small beach backed by trashcans and concrete.
Bits of torn paper scrape the sand; the sky
Supports a few gulls. Words seem obsolete

In settings such as these. The salt gusts blow
The scent of marijuana up our way.
No bathers in these tides, and, yes, I know
I've written nothing in three months. Friends say

That there's still gold in modernist motifs—
But I've learned what too much self-scrutiny
Does to the spirit. Secondhand beliefs,
The palpitating soul: how carefully

We shelter and array these. Two jets fade
West of the low sun, and the Golden Gate
Shines with a kind of neo-gothic pride,
A bright memorial of the welfare state.

Seaward, tugboats and freighters lead and bear
The commerce of the Far East and Marin;
But gulls shriek at a distance, as if aware
Of the grim age the tide is bringing in.

JOGGING IN THE PRESIDIO

A laughable and solitary art,
This running. Yet as I head toward the rise,
The snap of gravel underfoot is part
Of loveliness—of wind, Van Ruisdael skies,

That grove of eucalyptus just passed through,
And, here, the mobile shade of fir and pine.
Though wayside skeptics eye me, I pursue
Nothing particular, nothing that's mine,

But merely leaves brought down by a hard rain
Last evening, the clear wind the swallows ride,
And the grass over which my shadow bends
Evenly uphill as I hit my stride.

California Street, 1975–76

The studio was too dark and small,
The building too Victorian,
High-ceilinged and impractical—
Or so I thought when I moved in.

Yet out back was a garden sweet
With laurel, pyracantha, rose,
And a stone Bacchus stood knee-deep
In wild thyme, shouldering a green hose.

And when night came, the studio changed.
I'd light a fire whose glow would fall
Upon the books and journals ranged
Shelf upon shelf against the wall.

The room grew larger then, more still.
I'd watch the logs burn down to ash,
Each holding its smooth shape until
Collapsing with an orange crash.

Outside the light rain turned to mist,
That dampness sheltering my retreat.
When a car passed, its tires hissed
Over the slick black lamplit street.

Sometimes those nights I'd take a walk
Around the neighborhood, and stop
By daytime haunts: the Deli on Clay,
The Corner Store, Sam's Flower Shop.

Or pausing by a globed streetlamp,
I'd breathe the wetness and the light,
My collar turned against the damp
Till I was wholly of the night.

Last Night as You Slept

The clock's dial a luminous two-ten,
Its faint glow on pillow and sheet,
I woke—and the good fatigue and heat
We'd shared were gone; and I, sensing again

Distance as chill as the light on the shades,
Was so uncertain, love, of our rest
That I woke you almost as I drew my chest
Against the warm wings of your shoulder blades.

A DEVOTIONAL SONNET

Lord, pity such sinners. Monday afternoon
Is not the proper time for Augustine.
My saints are porcelain, chipped clair de lune,
Books and white wine. But please don't intervene:
My chastity, unwitting though it is,
Is real; nor have I worshipped bitterness.
Jobless and on the loose, my share of bliss
Is simply that I've felt what I confess.

And what absolves me? This chilled Chardonnay,
Letters postmarked from Cambridge and Vermont,
And You, who will restrain me if I stray
Too far from love I both reject and want.
And should this be "interpreted disease,"
Yours are such sinners, such apologies.

MORNINGS IN A NEW APARTMENT

Neither the pauper nor the nouveau riche,
You waken to the novelties of dawn:
Velveeta cheese suffices here for quiche;
Your boots, one doubled over, rest upon
A fruit crate shared by Zane Grey and Stendhal.
And should you mourn the cherubs on the ceiling
(Smirking and fat, whose latex robes are peeling),
Remember that location, after all,

Is just an opportunity you trace,
A summons to adventure and delight.
Note, then, the asters on the mantelpiece;
Dust off the candlesticks whose verdigris
Catches the sun. So casual a grace
Might save you as you are. Indeed, it might.

RURAL COLLOQUY WITH A PAINTER

By noon, as I recall, the sky was clear,
The meadow drying in the wind and sun.
The dark boughs of a hillside spruce in motion,
We sat on your porch drinking Hires root beer
As you expatiated on the notion—
Your cherished old Whiteheadean ideal—
That form and movement are, or can be, one.

From a black granite shelf, your spaniel watched
Crows angle toward the wood. Serene, you praised
Eakins and Hopper, your hands giving shape
To what you said: *The logical escape*
From all the self's excesses is the real.
Then, with facetious gravity, you raised
Your glass and, in a long gulp, downed your drink.

And I, although not quite convinced, could think
That those wildflowers whose names I'd never know,
The spruce, the hillside, and the field below
Would offer their concurrence if they could.
Even if form and movement were not one,
It hardly mattered much there in the sun.
I think that Whitehead might have understood.

ONE MORNING

One morning, rubbing clear the windowpane,
He grows coherent. The dark aimless rain

Becomes, abruptly, perfect thought; the jeans
Draped from the chair, that vase, the magazines

Scattered on his desk seem to draw within
Some final syllable. And who he's been,

Or what, no longer counts. The hours dispose
The silence and the light, advance and close

Into his will alone. Force? Harmony?
It is his time, whose coming even he

Could never quite imagine—simple, clear,
And endlessly complete. Right now. Right here.